Words of Certitude

D0905490

An inspiring collection of insights from the sermons, talks, articles, and books on Pope John Paul II. He responds to challenging modern-day questions about God, death, sorrow, sin, conscience, truth, work, prayer, love, and the Christian family. These short, pensive passages reflect the Pope's deep spiritual meditation on human life and serve as the perfect source for one's own meditations and prayers.

WORDS OF CERTITUDE

WORDS OF CERTITUDE

Excerpts From His Talks and
Writings
As Bishop and Pope

POPE JOHN PAUL II

Phoenix Press

WALKER AND COMPANY
New York

Large Print Edition published by arrangement with Paulist Press

Copyright © 1979 by Piero Gribaudi Editore, Torino. English translation Copyright © 1980 by The Missionary Society of St. Paul the Apostle in the State of New York

Library of Congress Cataloging in Publication Data

John Paul II, Pope, 1920–
  Words of certitude.

  Translation of: Parole di certezza.
  1. Meditations.   2. Large type books.   I. Title.
[BX2185.J6413   1984]   230′.2   84-16495
ISBN 0-8027-2477-9 (lg. print)

This edition printed in 1986.

Printed in the United States of America

First Large Print Edition, 1984
Walker and Company
720 Fifth Avenue
New York, New York 10019

10 9 8 7 6 5 4 3 2

Contents

Preface

THIS volume gathers together, according to themes, thoughts and reflections of Karol Wojtyla, Pope John Paul II, on some of the deepest and most abiding questions of the human spirit, questions that are just as pressing in our own day as in any time in human history. This is not an original essay, for all of the quotations printed here have been taken from texts already published or from talks given elsewhere. They are the fruit of many years of teaching, preaching and pastoral care of one of the most remarkable leaders of our time. Set apart in striking simplicity they speak to us in their own direct way and make a powerful impression.

In light of the impact that his visits as pope have made in Mexico, Poland, Ireland and the United States, it has seemed valuable to include a supplement, now found as Part Four, with selections from his homilies and talks given on these pilgrim journeys. The choices have been mine, but the criteria for the decisions have been simply whether the passages in question shared the same tone and spirit as the earlier texts adopted for Parts One to Three in the Italian original.

As originally published by Gribauda in Italian, the book was titled *Parole di Certezza*, "Words of Certainty," and was part of a series called "Values and Fidelity," whose purpose was "to fill the emptiness of heart afflicting modern man by providing him with points of reference for a human and Christian commitment that is really alive."

I wish to thank Mr. Anthony Buono for his labor in doing the basic translation of this volume. In places, I have revised the translation with an eye to more inclusive language. The Italian uses *l'uomo*, "man," in almost every line and in every conceivable context. It would have been inaccurate to the translation and to the power of the pope's thought to have merely removed all evidence of "man" as sexist language. In many cases the term has a substantial, philosophical and theological weight in his use which becomes banal and questionable by substituting "individual" or "person" or similar words. But where he addresses all of us in hortatory and pastoral terms, I have usually employed more appropriate wording than "man" alone.

Such a collection of brief quotations, taken out of their original settings, serves best to stimulate our own spiritual reflections by their freshness and originality. They by no means exhaust, or substitute for the value of the original sermons, talks, and essays from which they are taken. In the original Italian edition, however, these excerpts do not indicate the source from which they come. Since no comprehensive index or full translation of all the pope's writings and talks is yet available, we have presented the text as it was produced. The additions in our supplement from the talks given by the pope on his journeys to foreign countries, on the other hand, do note the occasion and place of each selection. These have been taken from diocesan newspapers and other news sources. For those who wish to find the fuller text of the pope's remarks, I would recommend one of the books collecting his talks that are now beginning to appear, or to consult the various issues of *Origins*, a weekly documentary service published by the United States Catholic Conference, in which all of the talks have been reprinted at the time of the individual trips of the pope.

Lawrence Boadt, CSP
Editor

Introduction

NEVER before has man found himself alone and lost in the face of the crisis which assails him in this society that consumes and scorches everything.

Who am I? Where am I going? Who is God? What is freedom? What is the reason for death? How do I bear witness to my faith? How must I act so as not to be ashamed of myself?

This book gathers together the most beautiful responses that Pope John Paul II gives—without tremor in his voice, and with strength of doctrine and solidity of truth—to the many questions that torture us.

This volume leaves its mark. For no one like Pope John Paul II has known how, in such a short time, to fill the emptiness of values which have overtaken us; not in a consoling manner, not through "going back," but specifically by calling for a rigorous and coherent renewed fidelity to God and man.

All who are tired of vague and stereotyped formulas and are looking for solid and certain values in our civilization will find in these pages a point of reference to provide a basis for their specific reality as children of God.

One

Certainty of God

As far as I am concerned,
the principal proof
of the existence of God
is given by the joy which I experience
in thinking that God exists.

René Le Senne

God

In the Presence of the Great Heart

I RECALL a lengthy discussion with a certain scientist, an eminent scholar and a man of great rectitude, who told me: "From the point of view of my science and its method, I am an atheist . . ." It is that same person who, in all sincerity, once wrote to me: "Every time I find myself in front of the majesty of nature, of mountains, I feel that he exists!"

I will never forget the impression that a Russian soldier made on me in 1945. The war had just ended when a military man knocked on the door of the Seminary of Cracow. When I asked, "What do you want?" he replied that he wanted to enter the seminary. I came away from our encounter with the perception of a great truth: God succeeds in mysteriously penetrating the human mind even under the extremely unfavorable conditions wherein he is systematically denied. The man who spoke with me had never entered a church. In school and later at work he had constantly heard the declaration that God does not exist. Yet despite it all he was repeating: "But I always knew that God existed . . . and now I would like to learn something about him . . ."

Man possesses the concept of infinity. He uses it in his scientific work—for example, in mathematics. Hence, the infinite finds in him, in his intelligence, adequate room for receiving the one who is Infinite.

It is this God whom the Trappist professes in his silence or even the Camaldolese. It is to him that the bedouin in the desert turns when it is time for prayer. And possibly so does the Buddhist, concentrating in his contemplation, which purifies his thoughts and prepares the way to nirvana.

The silence which at times seems to separate us from God also constitutes a special act of the vital union between God and the human spirit. The Church of our day has become particularly aware of this truth.

We come to know God by our encounter with him, and vice versa, he encounters us in the act of coming to know him. We encounter God when we open up to him with the inner gift of our human "I," to accept and reciprocate God's gift.

The human intelligence, no matter from what premise it starts, will in the final analysis always in some way confirm the truths of creation.

The contingent being is not a necessary being. The created being is not an absolute. But it is the goodness of the created being that reveals love as the motive of creation.

A single logic rules all of creation from the very beginning. It is a "logic of love," which may perhaps be equated with the logic of which Pascal spoke: "The heart has its own reasons." Exactly, the heart! Throughout the whole narrative of Genesis we hear the beating of a heart!

We do not have before us a great builder of the world, a Demiurge. We are in the presence of the great heart.

Today we can understand neither Sartre nor Marx without first having read and meditated upon the first three chapters of Genesis to their fullest depths. They constitute the key for understanding today's world at its very roots.

The dialogue with today's world is a dialogue of salvation, and its beginnings must be sought precisely in the covenant, that is, in that fundamental initial dialogue of God with man. Why? Perhaps because all humanity reveals ever more deeply the roots of its existence on earth. And possibly because we are today at the threshold of a new eschatology. And eschatology is understood fully only when we go back to the beginnings, to the most basic problems which implicitly conceal the traces of the ultimate truths.

The covenant arises from the great heart, from God's love for us. At the same time, the covenant is constituted on truth; it is rooted in that which is real, that which is true.

When God says: "I will put enmity between you and the woman, and between your seed and her seed . . ." (Gn 3:15), these words in no way deny the great heart so profusely spoken about in the early chapters of Genesis. These words merely affirm that that heart—and that heart alone—lies outside the dramatic contrast, the opposition between good and evil; that that heart is beyond these, thus constituting the ultimate foundation of the good.

Who is this God, who is even greater than the world, the world that "fell into the bondage of sin"? Who is this God who is even greater than time and space and the history of man?

During Advent we recite the great antiphons which express in marvelous fashion the most noble hopes of the people of God. But at the moment when he arrives, all the antiphons unexpectedly fall into the most profound silence. And this silence involves even the human mind, its projects and calculations. One certainty alone remains: "God is totally Other."

He has in himself nothing of the soldier of fortune or king; he is defenseless, just as his mother; . . . he is defenseless and without a roof, and very soon afterward he is an exile. During his whole life he shared the lot of the poorest in Israel and for thirty years he remained in the shadow of this silence of Nazareth, without possessing any instrument which would assure him of earthly power and dominion. "Truly you are a hidden God—O Savior" (Is 45:15).

Thus, Christ's coming into the world constitutes the revelation of an economy which is completely unique, proper only to God. It is a question of a divine economy whose font is constituted by the Father, the Son, and the Holy Spirit. This font overflows into the water of the great river which extends over the confines of the whole earth, which permeates the history of the world. "From within him who believes in me there will arise streams of living water" (Jn 7:38). Living water runs through the history of every man, passes through his heart and his works, without his awareness and despite all his exclusively temporal plans.

The one who has been sent by the Father manifests himself to our eyes in a radical fashion as a poor person all through his life. The "quantifier" of the divine economy —if we may so speak—is completely different from that used by the world. It is such, because God himself is totally other.

By refusing to recognize God as his beginning, man destroys the relationship that he should have with his last end and consequently destroys the whole order of his attitude toward himself, other men, and all created realities.

Fatherhood is the most profound mystery of God.

Union with God is the completion of our spiritual life. With such a completion the human being reaches reality at its depths. God is absolute completion of existence and whoever is united with him is consolidated in this completeness by means of knowledge and love.

The more we come to know God's love for us, the more we understand the rights which God possesses over our person and our love.

When we receive God in the Eucharist, it is he who receives us. The God of infinite majesty is close to us! In this wonderful sacrament he allows us to touch him, to feed on him: He receives each of us, helps us to lift ourselves up ever anew, and confirms the great dignity that is ours.

Christ

God is Born and the Powers Tremble

HUMANITY is associated with God above all because Jesus Christ, Son of God and Redeemer of mankind, is human. Continuously being created and increasing around him are the "people of God," the society of humanity with God.

Christ is the one who proclaims the divine truth and also the one who makes manifest our dignity connected with the truth: with a truth honestly pursued, contemplated in the heart, accepted with joy as the greatest treasure of the human spirit, and witnessed before men by means of words and works.

Whoever sees Jesus sees the Father also. The church lives from this vision, left us by the Lord. This vision permeates the whole consciousness of the Church, constitutes her mission and her joy in the midst of difficulties, and has become the foundation for her faith, hope and love.

Thus, nowadays man often does not know what he hears within himself, in the depths of his soul, in his heart. And thus he is often uncertain about the meaning of his life on this earth. He is assailed by doubt which turns into despair. Let, therefore, I beg and implore you with humility and trust, let Christ speak to man. He alone has words of life, indeed of eternal life.

Do not be afraid to receive Christ and accept his power! Help the Pope and all those who want to serve Christ and, with the power of Christ, serve each individual and all humanity! Do not be afraid! Open —in fact, fling wide—the doors to Christ! Open to his power the confines of states, economic as well as political systems, the vast fields of culture, civilization, and development. Do not be afraid!

Our age invites us, impels us, obliges us to look to the Lord and immerse ourselves in a humble and devout meditation on the mystery of the supreme power of Christ. The one who was born of the Virgin Mary, the son of a carpenter—as was believed—the Son of the living God as Peter confessed, came to make all of us "a kingdom of priests."

Through the incarnation of the Son of God the great dignity of human nature has been highlighted and through the mystery of the Redemption the price of every individual person has been revealed.

To the question: "Who is Jesus Christ for you?" a seminarian replied: "I want to cry out because we can be born again in God. And therefore I celebrate the day of your birth, Christ, as my birth."

"God is born and the powers tremble.
The Lord of heaven is despoiled.
The fire is banked and the splendor is
    dimmed.
The Infinite accepts limits.
Undervalued—invested with glory.
The immortal—the king of the ages."

The above is a stanza from a Polish Christmas hymn which contains, in my judgment, a tremendous expression of the mystery of God incarnate. A mystery which embraces contrasts: the light and the darkness of the night, the infinity of God and the limitations of man, glory and abasement, immortality and mortality, divinity and the poverty of man. In that moment something takes place that has no parallels in the history of man.

Christmas: this is the night of our greatest exaltation; in it we find our birth.

The manger: the first place of the encounter between God and men.

The one who was born in all our weakness was born in order to help me to be human, to give me the power to be a human being. Indeed to be fully human signifies to become a child of God because the Son of God has become human.

Our age has a special need of Christ, the one who before Pilate said: "For this have I come into the world, to bear witness to the truth" (Jn 18:37); the one who embraces, confirms, and guarantees the essential profile of the "mystery of man" combined with

14

its relation to the truth, with the responsibility of the truth, with the witness borne to the truth.

Jesus seals his witness with his blood. And this is the heritage he has bequeathed to the Church.

Varying programs exist for the progress of civilization, for the social and cultural progress; all in diverse ways, indicate the paths of this progress. However, among all of them, the cross of Christ is the unique place and the unique mode of God in which man is ever "exalted."

On the cross our exaltation toward the heights is incessantly activated. Because it is God who lifts and bears the weight—let us not be disturbed.

All humanity, the Church and the world, the past, the present, and the future unite in the most profound and complete silence of adoration before the fact that "Christ became obedient for us unto death" (Phil 2; 8). That silence is the attitude most suited to the human spirit, its most exact "word."

On Golgotha man died on the cross. But on Golgotha, through the medium of the cross, man was also born.

The Sacrifice of the cross is the point in history when every individual is, so to speak, conceived anew.

The mystery of the cross of Christ goes beyond human intelligence and the human way of understanding things. At the same time, that mystery always returns in our reflection on the world, on God, on ourselves, on good, on evil, and on eternity. And we can always contemplate a new aspect of the same ineffable mystery. "The cross stands while the world turns."

Christ's death on the cross, as an act of supreme love, has a redemptive character and at the same time a character of the bridegroom's love. Jesus said to the apostles on Holy Thursday: "I am going away . . . and I will come back to you . . ." (Jn 14:3; 14:18). Certainly, on the day of Pentecost the apostles experienced the meaning of these words: Christ has returned—or rather he has remained.

The cross is not dialectic. On the cross one cannot say falsehoods. The cross says the whole truth . . . The truth that is proclaimed from the cross is a truth of love. God loves—the Father loves. He has expressed this love by sacrificing his Son. And the Son, in this love, whose expression he became, has gone to the very end, because he has accepted the cross and on the cross he has remained with us.

"And know that I am with you all days even to the end of the world" (Mt 28:20).

"I am . . .," but not in a mere remembrance, or in literature or in commentaries.

"I am," I am present in the sacrament of my death, the very death through which I left you.

I am going and I will return continually through that same death.

I am "truly, substantially and sacramentally" (DS 883/1651).

I am . . . the power of the Holy Spirit, the power from on high, which in an invisible way fashions and maintains the Church.

That "return" of Christ in the Holy Spirit has about it the character of the return of the bridegroom. It is a divinely generous donation. It is not possible to think otherwise when in the Church there is celebrated the great sacrament of the Body and Blood of Christ. It is a gift of his person and his act, that conclusive definitive, redemptive, and hence saving act. It is a gift which expresses love, not only the love of the Lamb of God on the cross, but also the love of the bridegroom, for whom the Church, and even every person, every human soul "in Christ," becomes a bride.

Jesus Christ must triumph. Every time that his grace overcomes the forces of evil in us, he restores our youth, widens the horizons of our hope, and fortifies the energies of our trust.

The silence of God characterizes—according to some—our times and creates a particularly difficult climate. But we must ask ourselves if this is really true. God has said everything when he has spoken in the Son, his eternal Word. The sole question is whether the power of the Word heard is equivalent to the fullness of the Word pronounced to the specifications of all the ages.

Mary

The Earth is Full of Her Maternity

THE Mother of God's Son is for us the Mother of God's grace, and it is in the perspective of grace that he fulfills her maternity.

The earth is full of the Maternity of Mary, and souls are also replete with it.

If his Mother had not given her consent, Christ would never have undergone his torment nor would he have died on the cross—in short, he would not have redeemed us.

We have the right to reason in this way if we admit that the Son of God as Son of Man was completely subjected to the will of his Mother; without this submission he would not have been able to be for us an admirable example of the fourth commandment.

When the angel greets Mary with the words, "Hail, full of grace!" in a certain sense—but one that is nonetheless real—God awaits her personal choice. For freedom is the indispensable condition of love and of self-giving to God.

If in a determinate moment of history there arises a particular need to entrust oneself to Mary, such a need stems from the rediscovery of the whole divine economy to its very depths.

The Church, the people of God, is at the same time the Mystical Body of Christ. St. Paul has likened the Church to the human body in order to express better her life and her infinity. She is the mother who imparts life and unity to the human body.

Mary, by the power of the Holy Spirit, has given unity to Christ's human body. Therefore our hope is directed today in a particular way to her, in this age of ours when the Mystical Body of Christ finds its most complete recomposition in unity.

May Mary grant us that faith with which she chanted her "Magnificat"; may we share her faith, which is such that it can render us strong and unwavering in our adherence to Christ.

O Mother, you know what it means to hold in your arms the dead body of a Son, the one to whom you gave life; spare all the mothers of this earth the death of their children, torments, bondage, the destruction of war, persecutions, concentration camps, and prisons!

Death

The Mystery of a New Life

MAN who according to the laws of nature is "condemned to death," man who lives within the perspective of the annihilation of his body —that man exists at the same time within the perspective of the future life and is called to glory.

From the moment when we, because of sin, were separated from the tree of life (Gn 3), earth became a cemetery. There are as many graves as there are people. A great planet of tombs!

Among all the tombs spread out over the continents of our planet, there is one in which the Son of God, the man Jesus Christ, conquered death with death.

The tree of life revealed itself anew to us in the Body of Christ: "If anyone eats this bread he will live forever; and the bread that I will give is my flesh for the life of the world" (Jn 6:51).

A life conscious of the mystery of Christ finds its affirmation in a certain sense in death: "I desire to be dissolved and to be with Christ" (Phil 1: 23), that is, I desire a dimension of life which has been begun in me by Christ. The Christian is conscious of this anticipation. And even this constitutes the specific aspect of his death.

Every dying man bears in himself the mystery of a new life, which Christ has brought and grafted onto humanity. Every human death, without exception, has this dimension, even if the dying man or those who surround him could be unaware of this reality. It does not result from our awareness but from the plan and revelation of God.

Just as all have been sanctified "in Christ Jesus," so even the significance of our death lies in prolonging this "life in Christ." "For if we live, we live for the Lord; if we die, we die for the Lord. Therefore, whether we live or die, we are the Lord's" (2 Cor 5:6).

With the cross of Christ, death became the beginning of life; it became the exuberant font of the new life. This is the substance of the divine mystery which animates the Church and humanity.

Even if someone does not choose his own death, still by choosing his own form of life he, in a certain sense, chooses in this perspective even his own death.

Man is a "being on the way to death," states a German existentialist. Man is a "being on the way to glory," affirmed the one who was born in a stable and died on the cross like a slave.

Sorrow

The Ineffable Majesty of God

IN suffering we seem to attain a better grasp of the fundamental meaning of the proportions which in general escape our attention. We seem to experience more deeply the fragility of our existence and hence the mystery of our creation, the responsibility for life, the sense of good and evil, and finally the ineffable majesty of God.

Anyone who passes through the great catechesis of the cross, anyone who contemplates its mystery, cannot come away from the cross empty-handed.

He must feel that he possesses hands ready for great tasks, and possesses a heart ready for genuine love, and a whole life worthy of being lived freely, for his own liberation and that of his neighbor, his family, his children, and his country.

Suffering configures you to Christ, who alone can give meaning and value to every act of our lives.

Christ is found in the hearts of the sick and in the hearts of the "Samaritans" who serve the sick.

The nearer suffering comes, the more I must experience it alone.

I open myself, I place myself before the Lord, in all inner truth and I ask, "Examine me, O Lord!" It is a bit similar to what a sick person does with his doctor. "Examine my heart!"

But not only, "Examine me, O Lord!" I do not seek only a diagnosis or a species of "divine skill." I ask, "Put me to the test!" Putting to the test is not only the beginning of awareness. It constitutes in a certain sense its fullness and the foundation of a more mature verification.

How many times someone offers God his pretexts! Once it is a case of suffering, another time it is a case of the injustices or even of all the evil in the world. But when he turns his gaze to the cross he cannot fail to be perturbed.

A strange thing happens: it is as if the one hanging on the cross, Jesus, in an instant justifies all; it is as if in that instant he justifies God himself before man!

Egoism, of the senses or the sentiments, can be hidden only for a short time, camouflaged in the folds of a fiction called with seemingly good faith "love." But the fragility of this construction is destined fatally to manifest itself one day. And it is one of the major sufferings to see love reveal itself as something other than what it was believed to be.

Once again we cry out loudly, "Respect man. He is the image of God."

Tenderness is the art of "listening" to the whole man, the entire person, all the movements of his soul, even the most hidden ones, thinking always of his true good.

Sin

The Reality of a Distorted
Revelation of God

FROM the very beginning of the Bible it becomes clear that our history and with it the history of the world, to which we are united through creation, will be subjected to the dominion of the word and the anti-word, of the Gospel and the anti-Gospel.

The Father of lies does not present himself as denying the existence of God. He does not deny his existence and omnipotence which are expressed in creation. He points directly to the God of the covenant.

The denial of God without reservation is impossible . . . even in Satan himself. Instead, the destruction of the truth concerning the God of the covenant, concerning the God who creates out of love, who in love offers humanity the covenant in Adam, who out of love places before us exigencies which touch the very truth of our created being—the destruction of this truth is, in Satan's discourse, total.

To Satan, who declares: "*You will become like God*, acquiring the knowledge of good and evil," the "divinity" of the human person is hardly important. He is only interested in communicating, transmitting his rebellion, to us—that is, the attitude by which he, Satan, has defined himself: "I will not serve."

Satan does not succeed in conquering in everything, that is, he reveals himself incapable of sowing in us a total rebellion, the one which he bears in himself. But he does succeed in prompting us to turn toward the world, deviating more and more in the direction away from the destiny to which we were called.

From that moment the world will remain the field of our temptation, the field of turning one's back on God, in different ways and in varying degrees; a field of rebellion against instead of collaboration with the creator; a field where human pride is nurtured instead of the quest for God's glory.

The world as the field of the struggle between man and God, of the opposition of the created being to his creator—this is the grand drama of history, of myth, and of civilization.

If we wish to grasp the problem of the denial of God at its roots, we must come back to the reality of Satan.

One has the impression that in the measure in which the world fashioned by man advances, there grows in him at the same time the weariness of being human and the responsibility for good and evil.

The history of events—perhaps especially in our day—presents an ever-greater distance between the huge increase in what man possesses and his moral deficiency, a deficiency in what he is. We can safely say that man in the sphere of what he is does not increase what he possesses.

Sin is a profoundly human fact in which man realizes himself wrongly in relation to himself, to others, and to the world.

The world is subjected to the gravity of the body which tends downward through inertia. Precisely in this gravity lies the passion of the Crucified: "You are from below. I am from above" (Jn 8:23).

Two

Human Certainty

What you must dare:
is to be yourself.
What you could obtain:
that the greatness of life
be mirrored in you
to the extent of your "purity."

Dag Hammarskjold

Human Value

The Glory of God is Man Alive

Every created being,
through the sole fact that it is,
and through the fact that it is such a
        created being,
manifests in a certain measure
the absolute perfection of the being
that is God.

The glory of God is the primary norm of
reality, and its realization will govern the
fulfillment of everything. The glory of God
is living man; the glory of God is that man
lives.

Even history rejoices when it can manifest
the true glory of the human person.

Christ knows what is in us. He alone knows
it.

We must recall and repeat for everyone in our day: The bridegroom is with you! You are loved even to the full and definitive giving. This is what Jesus has left us as an inheritance: love for every human being. It is a patrimony which seems poor but is in reality the most powerful of all. For what do we seek if not to be loved? What gives fundamental meaning to our existence if not this? We are poor, but we are rich. The bridegroom is with you!

There is a right autonomy of earthly realities and an erroneous one.

In the first covenant man was called not only to obedience to God the creator but also to "justice." Man who has attained great progress, achieved a great civilization and an even more perfect technology, as has modern man, seems to be even more "unjust" in his encounters with God the creator. It is here that the ancient drama of human temptation unfolds between secularism and secularization.

While secularization attributes the "just" and due autonomy to earthly realities, secularism proclaims instead that the world is going to be taken away from

God! And then? It will be given entirely to man! But can the world really be given to man in any greater fashion than it was given to him at the beginning of creation?

Creatures are the work of God. And the fact that he called them into existence demonstrates an act of his creation.

Man, independently of his extreme littleness, his great weakness, and all his deficiencies, is great. Behind him is God. God has become man.

A pilgrimage . . . we, by the very fact of being persons, by our intelligence and our freedom, which distinguish us from all other creatures of the visible world, cannot think of our own life in any other way. The analogy of pilgrimage and the comparison with the way correspond more fully to what we are: wayfarers, pilgrims of the absolute.

At the base of the truth about humanity, professed by the Church even "to the shedding of blood," there is the profound conviction that we are irreducible to matter alone. If we are masters over matter, we are such only as a result of the "element of the spirit" (cf. Rom 8:23) which we bear in ourselves, and which is expressed in conscience and in freedom—that is, in our activity.

Thus, we could even accept a part of the truth contained in the affirmation that "work creates man." Yes, it creates—but because it is a work, that is, an activity, a "praxis," of the individual, "an act of the person."

God, as the end of all creatures, does not require that they deny themselves as creatures, diminishing their immanent perfection. Instead he reinforces them in their perfection.

The same is true in our encounters with man. God, as the end of man, does not divert him in the slightest from his perfection, from the fullness of humanity. Rather he places and strengthens him in it even more forcibly.

Man conquers himself. Man must conquer himself.

Man conquers himself by tending toward God and thus overcomes even the limits imposed on him by creatures, by space and time, and by his contingency. The transcendence of the person is directly connected with the reference to the one who constitutes the fundamental base for all our judgments concerning being, good, truth, and beauty.

The Gospel of Jesus Christ has revealed to the human spirit its just dimensions.

> The Gospel is always, in all times,
> the revelation of the living God
> in its "opening out" to us.

The dimension of the "sacred," the "sacred" values—this is the highest and definitive sphere of human life as well as the sphere of our fullest self-realization. We realize ourselves more fully in this dimension. Contemplating the sacral values, having familiarity with them, we affirm ourselves more fully.

The spiritual man is at the same time the interior man and the complete man.

The Holy Spirit speaks through the testimony of all creatures, giving them the voice to speak.

The "Gift from on high," the Holy Spirit, restores to all persons, to all human relationships, to matrimony, to the family, to the diverse social circles, to nations and states the fundamental meaning of gift and of being "given."

The world issuing from the hands of the creator bears in itself the profound structure of a gift. To be something created means to be "given."

It is necessary to measure the human person with the yardstick of the spirit.

Everywhere there is a need for people of great spirit.

There is need for this type of individual in offices, on university chairs, in episcopal sees, and in parish services.

But there is also need for such people in the family circle; they are necessary in the places of daily work.

Everywhere there is need for a person of great spirit.

We are called to familiarity with God, to intimacy and friendship with him. God wants to be near us. He wants to make us share his plans. He wants to make us share his life. He wants to make us happy with his happiness.

This requires that we be "available."

Man
is not only
the author
of his own acts
but also
in a certain sense
the creator of himself.

In the realm of what he is, man adds nothing of what he has.

We can be perfected only within the framework of the order of the entire world, of all the beings and all the goods contained in it.

Man is a searching being. All his history confirms this. Even the life of each of us bears it out.

Many are the fields in which man seeks

and inquires and then finds, and sometimes after finding begins to seek anew.

Among all these fields in which man manifests himself as "a searching being," there is one which is the most profound. It is the field which penetrates most intimately into the very humanity of the human being. And it is the one most united to the meaning of all human life.

Man is the being who searches for God.

We would be discredited if we did not feel small in the face of authentic greatness.

With what veneration must the apostle of Christ pronounce this word: human!

Life

The Orientation Toward God

THE life of any man, of anyone who is on earth, can be computed by the measure of the time that elapses between the hour of his birth and the hour of his death. Faith tells us . . . that the life of man is completed only in God.

The word "vocation" (from the Latin "vocare"—to call) signifies etymologically the call of one person on the part of another and the duty to respond to it . . . It is manifested by the commitment of one's whole life to the service of certain values. Every person must find this direction, on the one hand ascertaining what he bears within himself and could give to others, and on the other hand becoming aware of what is demanded of him.

"Our eyes have seen the light . . ." With these words we conclude our days, thinking of the light that Christ is for us. And we offer thanks and express our joy in being able to walk in this Light, in being able to see our life and the life of others in this Light and ever anew fashion our life in it, spare no energy in its service, and live through it alone.

Sanctity consists in a life of concealment and humility: to know how to immerse oneself in the daily work of men, but in silence, without din of everyday gossip and without wordly echoes.

Commitment to sanctity entails austerity of life, serious control of one's pleasures and one's choices, a constant dedication to prayer, and an attitude of obedience and docility to the directives of the Church both in the doctrinal, moral, and pedagogical spheres and in the liturgical sphere.

Virtue is not something abstract and divorced from life, but on the contrary it has profound "roots" in life itself; it stems from life and fashions it.

The prudent person is not one who—as is often understood—knows how to arrange his life and knows how to derive the greatest profit from it. Rather it is the one who knows how to construct his life in accord with the voice of a right conscience and in accord with the demands of a just morality.

When our entire life is characterized day after day by a continuous religious reference, that is, when it is a life of faith, love, prayer, and silence, then "the orientation" toward God stems from the whole of our being and our activity.

Freedom and truth determine the spiritual imprint that marks the diverse manifestations of life and human activity. Above all, love has need of freedom; the commitment of freedom in a certain sense constitutes its essence. That "love" which does not have its proper source in freedom, that "love" which is not a free commitment since it is determined or the effect of compulsion, cannot be recognized as love; it contains none of love's essence.

Conscience

The "Royalty" of Man

OUR value must be measured by the yardstick of the moral good that we realize in life.

Obedience to one's conscience, which in turn obeys the divine law of love, brings it about that "to serve Christ in others is to reign" (LG 36).

In our obedience to our conscience is found the key to our moral greatness and the foundation of our "royalty."

Everyone must personally find an actual motivation for the good or evil of his actions. This is the function of his conscience.

Between the saint and the criminal
the difference consists
not only in actions,
but also in judgments:

in the fact as to how each one
judges himself.
The judgment of God,
as a rule
goes in accord
with the judgment
of conscience.

Conscience not only decides concerning the goodness or malice of our actions but also approves or disapproves of what we do. When it disapproves, it punishes and torments with remorse. And this is the fundamental temporal punishment in the purifying function willed by God. The remorse of conscience surpasses and condenses in itself the sense of every temporal punishment.

Flight before the law of nature is usually flight before personality.

The flight of human reason before a Superior Reason does not resist the test of life.

Through Christ's teaching in the face of sin, or better in the face of sinful people, there is always manifested a particular sense of the dignity or, we might say, the "royalty" of the person, who interiorly accepts the truth of his or her "sinfulness" and is converted.

This "royal" characteristic of humanity can be seen in the whole practice of penitence. The man who gets on his knees before the confessional because of his own failings at that very moment underscores his dignity as a man. Independently of how heavily his sins weigh on his conscience and of how much they have lowered his dignity, the very act of confession in truth manifests the particular dignity of man, his spiritual greatness.

Every confessor must—so to speak— "place himself on his knees" before the secrets of grace and the human conscience. Even if a confessor is a judge, director, or teacher of a brother or sister, he must exercise these attributes and these functions with the greatest respect for the "mystery of man," which finds its solution in the "mystery of Christ."

Truth

When Man is Himself

MAN is himself through the medium of the truth. The relation with the truth determines his humanity and constitutes the dignity of his person.

Every human being is born into the world to bear witness to the truth in accord with his or her particular vocation.

In us, truth is a function and a task of reason. And although there have been thinkers (Pascal and Scheler) who have emphasized the particular logic of the emotions ("logic of the heart"), we must state that emotive-effective reactions can both help and hinder attraction for a true good.

A man's maturity is based on his attitude toward the truth. Man has a right to the truth and man has a thirst for the truth!

Man wants to live in the truth and must live in the truth!

Truth forms our spiritual maturity. Truth is the basis for the dignity of the human person.

Man is himself because he relates to the truth, aspires to the truth, and seeks to know the truth. And when he knows it, when he has already known it, he becomes converted to it, works in accord with it, and bears witness to it in his social life.

Without such an attitude toward the truth, man does not realize his humanity. He remains undefined, vague, and inexpressive.

Particular truths are not enough for us even if in every field of human activity we seek the truth. Truth becomes for us a source of inspiration in work, in science. Nevertheless, the hunger for the truth in our souls goes further. The ultimate question is always a question about God, it is always a question about the meaning of human life, about the beginning and especially about the end of the road that we traverse on earth.

We must live by the truth, we must seek it, we must tend toward it. We cannot make any sense of or live by falsehood.

A climate of falsehood is always a climate against the human.

The Lord, who is the Way and the Truth, has the right to verify, in every moment of history, whether we are awake, that is, whether we are faithful to his truth and his love to the very end.

The truth of the knowledge of oneself, of the world, and of God; the truth of conscience, of science, and of faith—Jesus has told us clearly that this must not be denied before men (Mt 5:14–15) but that it must be openly acknowledged (Mt 10:32). The truth possesses a social and public dimension. Hence an individual must never be denied his or her right to the truth.

Everyone, up to a certain point or even in a total way, is called to bear witness to the truth. It is only then that a person's humanity finds its realization. We are complete and mature when we live by the truth and bear witness to it.

Thus even our social relations are true when we can bear witness to his truth, when in national life there is a place for the truth, when an individual with his truth must not hide himself in some part in caves; when that person is not denied the necessary means for him to express this truth; when there are not created conditions in which the truth becomes modeled according to the needs of a tendency that it alone has the right to exist, and there is a place only for it in social life.

The point of collision between the unjust civil power and the believer is not faith insofar as it is the truth hidden in the depths of the spirit as much as faith in its external profession, its witness. There are truly tragic situations in which a person is denied the right to bear witness to the Truth, and at the same time is obliged to profess what does not correspond to his or her most profound persuasions: that person is thus constrained to live in falsehood.

The right to the truth must be able to exist in every human being.

The worst situations are those which are not clear, those in which the boundaries between good and evil become blurred, and chaos reigns.

Work

Collaboration with God

ALL human work, all human production in whatever field, forms the human personality; however, it does so not through its objective content —that is, its product, but rather through moral value which in all of our activity, in our "praxis," constitutes a human and personal element.

It is not only work which "makes man," but—if we want to be faithful to an exact analysis of the human person—we must clearly affirm that all our self-realization, self-creation, has its source in moral conscience, in our spiritual center.

If humanity wants to control an evolution which escapes from its hand, if it wants to withdraw from the materialistic temptation which gains ground in a desperate flight forward, if it wants to assure authentic development for men and peoples, it must radically review its concepts of progress which under diverse names have let spiritual values atrophy.

Work must be the means by which all creation is subjected to the dignity of the human being and child of God. Work offers the opportunity of committing oneself together with the entire community without resentments, without bitterness, without hatreds, but with the universal love of Christ which does not exclude anyone and embraces all.

Work enters in the balance-sheet of progress to the extent that it contributes to the development of the human sense. Work is the condition for the development of the human sense. But an individual's fullness of humanity is developed through truth and love. These substantial coefficients of development for humanity are closely connected among themselves.

Work is not a curse; it is a blessing of God who calls us to subdue the earth and transform it, so that with our intelligence and strength it may pursue the creative and divine work. I want to let you know, with all my soul and all my energies, that the scarcity of work grieves me, injustice grieves me deeply, conflicts grieve me, and ideologies of hatred and violence grieve me for they are not evangelical and inflict so many wounds on contemporary humanity.

We would create a barely habitable world if we were to look solely to have more and not think first and foremost of the person, of the worker, of his conditions as a human being and a child of God, called to an eternal vocation, and if we did not think about helping him be more.

I know the meaning of the obligation of daily work in dependence on others. I know its burdensomeness and its monotony. I know the needs of workers, their just requirements, and their legitimate aspirations. And I know how necessary it is that work never be alienating and frustrating but always correspond to the superior spiritual dignity of the human person.

Every man, but especially the one who lives from a burdensome work, must be guaranteed what his spirit lives on. It is not possible to make man a kind of robot to incentives! He is in fact greater than all calculations which take account only of the economic factor.

Work is not always easy, pleasant, and satisfying; sometimes it can be burdensome, devalued, poorly compensated, and even dangerous. It is thus necessary to remember that every work is a collaboration with God to perfect the nature created by him, and is a service to one's brothers.

It is therefore necessary to work with love and through love! Then the worker will be content and serene always. Even if the work is tiring, he will take up his cross with Jesus Christ and endure his work with courage.

Prayer

The Eternal in the Dimension
of a Moment

THE varying and disquieting phenomena of social life . . . are all rooted in a profound lack: a lack of the worship of God! The individual who does not honor God does not respect the human person either; he does not respect in our humanity what is in us from God.

Indeed the tension toward the truth is in us from God! If we destroy in ourselves our attitude of adoration toward God, then we also destroy what is most profound in ourselves, in our relation with ourselves, and in our relations with others.

Prayer is an act of hope.

Prayer is a constitutive element of human existence in the world, which is "to be toward God." At the same time, it is a kind of "being in the dimensions of God," an insertion—humble but courageous—into the profundity of the thought of God, of his mystery, and of his designs.

Prayer is finally in some way a "contact" with the very source of the divine power: will and grace.

Prayer is the strength of the weak and the weakness of the strong.

Prayer gives a meaning to all of life, in every moment, in every circumstance.

Prayer is the first expression of the interior truth of our humanity, the first condition of the authentic freedom of the spirit.

A pause devoted to true adoration has greater value and spiritual fruit than the most intense apostolic activity. This is the most urgent "contestation" that is to be opposed to a society in which efficiency has become an idol, on whose altar the same human dignity is frequently sacrificed.

The soul that lives in habitual touch with God and comes within the warm ray of his love knows how to guard itself skillfully from the temptation of particularisms and counter-oppositions, which create the risk of painful divisions; it knows how to interpret in the just light of the Gospel the option for the most poor and for every victim of human egoism, without yielding to socio-political radicalizations, which in the long run turn out to be inopportune, counter-productive, and themselves generative of new oppressions; it knows how to get close to people and to insert itself in the midst of the people putting into question its own religious identity.

For believers, it is by consenting to God's speaking to us that we can contribute more truthfully to the reinforcement of the awareness that every human being has his or her own destiny, and to the cognition that all rights derive from the dignity of the person who is solidly rooted in God.

Prayer unites us with God and makes us brothers and sisters.

The fact that we desire God, that we seek him even when we find him—this is an elementary kind of truth concerning ourselves, a kind of measure of humanity, a verification of God's greatness.

Prayer is always a marvelous reduction of eternity to the dimension of a concrete moment, a reduction of the eternal Wisdom to the dimension of human understanding, to the concrete mode of comprehending and listening, a reduction of the eternal Love to the dimension of the concrete human heart, which at times is not capable of deriving the riches from it and seems to break.

More than speaking of prayer, we should participate in the prayer of Jesus Christ himself.

Three

Certainty of Love

Every mystery of grace
is grafted on charity
and lives from charity,
which has a unique heart and protects
with the same piety
the body and soul of man,
his own now
and the eternal which is already in him.

Primo Mazzolari

Love

The Law of the Gift

The Gospel
is completely pervaded
by the category of the gift,
by the revelation of the gift.

In matrimony, in the family, in the world of culture, economy, and politics, in the international order—in all these fields we must always rediscover the law of the gift.

Love alone is constructive!

Human beings have a right to love. Just as it is not permitted to deny this right to a person who is human, so it is not permitted to deny this right to the person who is God. Rather there are many reasons to discover in this fact a sublime affirmation of human possibilities.

In love there are no accounts to balance, but we desire the greatest good for the person loved.

Love frees what is most noble in us. We thus find ourselves beyond justice and at the opposite pole to utilitarianism.

Love is more perfect than justice. And this is felt more than understood insofar as in the realm of love there are placed all the manifestations of the heart, of goodness, of dedication, and of sacrifice, whereas with justice are associated, more than others, cold ratiocination, firmness, and severity.

Good
renders us
highly dynamic,
freeing in us
the totality
of human possibilities.

Love is contrary to parsimony, contrary to hoarding, and prompts us to generosity.

Love plays an extraordinary importance in social life: it guards against rigidity, totalitarianism, and institutionalization.

66

Christianity—which has defined the power of love and continues to seek to make it, in the best way possible, ever more known to us, if not to make it radiate in the life of great and small societies—plays an immense role in this regard.

It is legitimate for man to want more for himself; such a tendency is not opposed to the commandment of love.

He is allowed to will more for himself not only in the sphere of spiritual goods but also in that of material goods, under the sole condition that, having more, he will give to others more than to himself.

Charity is the key to human prompting. An individual considered in his personal and social reality cannot be prompted in better fashion than by charity. This is the prompting in which someone is worth more because of what he is than because of what he has.

As long as material values are exalted, there is proclaimed what divides and leads to fighting; there is proclaimed divergence and conflict of interests. The essential communion of human interests is connected with the sphere of spiritual values.

Two systems of value: materialism and Christianity. Two ethics: the ethics of struggle and the ethics of love. Two ways and two solutions of human destiny in every dimension.

Love has other dimensions: it belongs to other ambients. In a certain sense, the laws of time, in relation to love, remain suspended . . . Love can be achieved in a short time, sometimes even in one act; one act is enough.

Education creates the human person in the spiritual, moral sense. If human existence is determinative right from its conception and from its birth—and its belonging to God is determined by the grace associated with the sacrament of holy Baptism—Christian education must unite one to the other in the conscious work of its whole life.

Every person should be educated and should educate himself in order to know how to live together in a just manner with others who are his neighbors and, in accord with the faith, brothers in the Son of God.

The Christian program of life includes justice and love as principles and virtues by which "we are recognized as disciples of Christ the Lord" (Jn 13:35).

Persons who love God without reserve are in a particular way capable of loving others and of giving themselves to them without personal interests and without limits.

The remembrance of illustrious personages of the past and their charitable activities will not substitute for real actions in this sphere. The glance backward has the significance of example; it has the significance of setting imitation going. Nevertheless, it is necessary in the meanwhile to note that such imitation consists in finding new ways in the practice of charity.

Jesus dies on the cross . . . We pause in silence at the threshold of what is most holy in the history of the world. An immense love, "God's Love unto the deprecation of self." In this context it is silence itself which speaks more. The Church is silent on Good Friday. We keep quiet because we lack suitable words.

To believe in love is difficult. Jesus Christ had to enter the world, pass through it and depart from it so that his whole passage might confirm, from beginning to end, the truth of love.

St. Augustine wrote: "My love is my burden." This is the definition of the burden which arises from contemplation of the cross of Christ. Love not only elevates but exalts and also obligates. And perhaps the burdens speak more of love than do the moments of ecstasy and spiritual impetus. "My love is my burden."

Love is the most complete realization of our possibilities. It is the maximum actuation of the person's intrinsic potentialities. The person finds in love the greatest fullness of his own being, of his own existence.

True love perfects the being of the person and realizes its existence.

Love is by nature reciprocal: the person who knows how to receive also knows how to give.

Love is realized in the most profound way when the person desires to cease belonging exclusively to himself in order to belong also to others. He renounces being independent and inalienable.

Love passes through this renunciation, guided by the profound conviction of leading not to a diminishment or an impoverishment, but on the contrary to an enrichment and an increase of the being of the person. It is a kind of law of ecstasy: to go out of self in order to rediscover in others an increase of being. (In no other form of love is this law applied with such great evidence as in nuptial love.)

The gift of oneself can have full value only if it is the part and the work of the will.

The person is a good to the extent that only love can dictate the proper and valid attitude in its regard.

Love exists *between* persons; it is social. It is a force which binds and unites, and its nature is contrary to division and isolation.

When a person is desired as a good in himself, it is necessary to wish that the person desired be effectively good, so that he may really be a good for whoever desires him. Not "I desire you as a good" but "I desire your good," "I desire what is a good for you."

In the desire for the infinite good for another "I" there is the germ of the whole creative impulse, an impulse toward the gift of the good to persons loved in order to make them happy. It is the "divine" aspect of love. Indeed, when a man wishes the infinite good for another, he wants God for him, because he alone is the objective fullness of the good and he alone can fill man with it.

To be able to believe in the other, to be able to think of him or her as a friend who cannot delude is, for the one who loves, a source of peace and joy. Peace and joy, the fruits of love, are closely bound up with its very essence.

In love there is a responsibility, one assumed toward the person who is drawn in to the closest communion of existence and action, and who, thanks to the gift of self, becomes in some measure our property. Consequently, we also assume a responsibility toward our love: is that love true, sufficiently mature and profound so as not to delude the immense trust of the other person and the hope born of his love that, by giving himself, he will not lose his own "soul" but, on the contrary, will find a greater fullness of being?

The responsibility for love is brought back, as we see, to the responsibility for the person; the former derives from the latter and returns to it. Precisely for this reason, it is an immense responsibility.

In love, we select a person so that we may find in that individual, so to speak, another "I"; it is as if we were to choose ourself in the other person, and the other in ourself.

While purely affective love is characterized by an idealization of the proper object, love founded on the value of the person makes us love him as he truly is: not the idea that we form of him but the real being. We love him with his virtues and his defects, and up to a certain point independently of his virtues and despite his defects.

Love never "is," but it "becomes" what the contribution of each of the persons and the depth of their commitment make of it.

From the viewpoint of educating to love, the following demand is imposed: it is necessary to *transform* sympathy into friendship and to *complete* friendship with sympathy. Sympathy must mature in order to become friendship, and this process normally demands reflection and time. But, on the other hand, friendship must be completed with sympathy; deprived of sympathy, friendship would remain cold and poorly communicative.

Sympathy is only a signal; it is never a perfect rapport between persons. It must find in us its proper foundation, taking friendship as its basis; it will make the climate and warmth of friendship flourish. Friendship and sympathy must compensate one another without becoming entangled. In this consists the "art" of education of love, the true "art of loving."

Love must be transparent: every act that manifests it must enable us to glimpse the recognition of the value of the person. Consequently, since the senses and the sentiments can generate the eroticism which deprives love of this transparency, in order to preserve its true character and objective aspect there is need for a special virtue: chastity.

To be chaste signifies to have a "transparent" attitude in encounters with a person of the opposite sex. Chastity is the "transparency" of interiority, without which love is not grand and cannot be such.

Love must seek!

Human love is also a struggle, a struggle for us and for our good.

Sexuality

From Impulse to Fecundity

L OVE owes to impulse its fecundity in the biological sense, but it must also be fecund in the spiritual, moral, and personal sense.

Persons capable of living in a group, capable of creating it, are without doubt well prepared to confer on their own family the character of a solidly united group, in which a positive atmosphere of life in common reigns.

In every situation in which we experience the sexual values of a person, love demands their integration into the value of the person, and indeed their subordination to that value. And in this precisely is manifested the principal moral characteristic of love: it is the affirmation of the person or it is not love.

Life confirms the value of a correct choice at the moment when sensuality and affectivity diminish or when sexual values cease to act. Then there only remains the value of the person, and the internal truth of love appears.

Nuptial love differs from all the other aspects and forms of love. It consists in the gift of the person. Its essence is the gift of self, of the proper "I."

Nuptial love can in no case be fragmentary or fortuitous in the interior life of the person. It always constitutes a particular crystallization of the total human "I," which because of this love resolves to conduct itself in this particular way.

The sexual element has a particular function in the formation of nuptial love. Sexual relations enable this love, limiting itself to a single couple, to acquire a specific intensity. And it is only in this way that it can overflow more expansively toward new persons who are the natural fruit of the conjugal love of man and woman.

Sensuality alone is not love and can also very easily become the opposite of love. In spite of this fact, it is necessary to acknowledge that in the man–woman relationship sensuality as a natural reaction before a person of the opposite sex is a component of conjugal love, of nuptial love. But it does not fulfill this function by itself.

The orientation toward the sexual values of the body, insofar as it is the object of pleasure, requires integration; it must be inserted into a valid attitude in encounters of the person, otherwise it will not be love.

We refuse to recognize the great value of chastity for love when we reject the integral and objective truth concerning the love of persons and replace it with a subjective fiction. On the contrary, when we admit this truth, we recognize the entire value of chastity, as a positive element of our life and essential symptom of the culture of the person, the nucleus of human culture.

Chastity does not lead to disdain for the body but indicates a certain humility. Now humility is the just attitude in encounters with every true greatness, even if it be my own. The human body must be humble in encounters with the greatness represented by the person, because it is precisely the latter that provides the true measure of a person. The human body must be humble in encounters with the greatness of love; it must be subordinate to love, and it is chastity which leads to this submission. Without chastity, the body is not subordinate to true love; on the contrary, it seeks to impose its own laws on love and to dominate it.

Love is love only when directed toward a person. When it is directed toward the body of a person it is not love, because the desire for pleasure which is manifested in it is substantially opposed to love.

The very moment when man participates in the order of nature and immerses himself, so to speak, in its impetuous processes, is the moment for him not to forget his proper nature as a person. For him, instinct alone does not resolve any problem; everything in him refers to his interiority, to his reason and his sense of responsibility, everything and especially that love which is the font of the development of the human race.

There exists a problem of educating in tenderness, comprised in the problem of "educating to love" in man and in woman, and consequently between them. It forms part of the problem of continence.

Women tend to become an object of love in order to be able to love. Men wish to love in order to be able to become an object of love.

The human body in itself is not impure and neither are the reactions of sensuality and sensuality itself; impurity arises from the will, which reduces the other person— because of his body and his sex—to the rank of an object of pleasure.

The body must be humble in the presence of human felicity. How often it pretends to be the only one to possess the key to its proper mystery!

In principle, love and procreation are indissoluble.

Courage and Faith

Let Us Not Allow Ourselves To Be Deprived of God

TO belong to the Church, to live in the Church, to be the Church is nowadays something very demanding. At times it does not necessarily cost clear and direct persecution but it may cost much disdain, indifference, and ostracism. Moreover, there is the ready and frequent danger of fear, weariness and insecurity. Do not let yourselves be conquered by these temptations.

Do not allow any one of these sentiments to lessen the spiritual vigor and energy of your "being Church," that grace which it is necessary to seek, to receive with great interior poverty, and to be ready to relive every day—and every day with greater fervor and more intensity.

Sanctity consists above all in living with conviction the reality of God's love, in spite

81

of the difficulties of history and one's own life.

Today, less than ever, it is possible to stop at a Christian faith which is superficial or of a sociological stripe. Times have changed . . . They call for a personal faith, that is, one which is sought with the desire for truth, so that it may then be lived integrally.

It is futile to moan about the wickedness of the times. As St. Paul already declared, we must overcome evil by doing good. The world esteems and respects the courage of ideas and the power of virtue.

Do not be afraid to refute words, acts, and attitudes that are not in conformity with Christian ideals. Be courageous in rejecting whatever destroys your innocence or impairs the freshness of your love for Christ.

To accept misunderstandings and persecutions without ever permitting a dichotomy between what is loved and what is believed —therein lies coherence. Here we are perhaps at the innermost nucleus of fidelity.

The virtue of strength requires always a certain overcoming of human weakness, especially fear. For humans by nature spontaneously fear dangers, misfortunes, and sufferings. Therefore it is necessary to seek individuals who are courageous not only on the fields of battle but also in the wards of a hospital or on beds of pain.

The virtue of strength proceeds hand in hand with the capacity for self-sacrifice.

We have need of strength to be human. Indeed the really prudent person is the one alone who possesses the virtue of strength; even as only the truly just individual is one who has the virtue of strength.

We cannot think of building a new world without being strong and courageous in overcoming the false ideas of fashion, the world's standards of violence, and the enticements of evil. All this requires that we break down the barriers of fear in order to bear our witness to Christ and to offer at the same time—the two realities are super-imposed on each other—an image of the true person, which is expressed uniquely in love, in the giving of self.

Our times have need especially of confessors and giving birth to confessors.

Today we must write modern "Acts of the Martyrs," the documents of confessors, so that we may be able to comfort one another, so that we may have news about one another, so that the evil inflicted on anyone because of his convictions, his faith, and his conscience may become our common cause.

We cannot be lukewarm or disenchanted; we must be confessors, because it is in our confession that there is manifested our whole relation to the truth, to God who is the truth.

Our confession of faith is in line with our human dignity. We can and must be proud of the fact that together with Christ we say: "I confess to you, Father, Lord of heaven and earth!" We must say it with him, with firmness and courage.

> Let us not allow ourselves to be
> deprived of God!
> Let us not allow anyone
> to take God away from our children,
> our youth,
> at any price.

Those would not be faithful . . . who would remain overly attached to accidental aspects of the Church, valid in the past, but now surmounted. Nor much less would they be faithful who, in the name of a poorly enlightened prophetism, would launch out into utopian and venturesome constructions of a so-called church of the future, discarnate from the present.

We must be faithful to the Church which was born once and for all from the plan of God . . . yet is born again every day, not from the people or from other rational categories, but from the same fonts from which it arose in its origins.

I will often be scolded for speaking about these things. And how could I remain silent? How could I not write? How could I fail to intervene?

Admittedly, heroism is not at the reach of all, but does not the refusal to aspire to it represent a defeat?

We are called in a particular way to bear witness to hope, that is, to aspire to what is above us, what goes beyond human measure, beyond our possibilities. We must want this, we must want it tenaciously, sometimes against our very self. The Latin motto has become well worn: "Contra spem sperare," which means what we must sometimes have hope "against hope."

Hope is often a "struggle against something." The Christian must be a person of hope since Christ places us before obligations which instinctively seem difficult and unrealizable. We have heard with what insistence he repeats: "Love your enemies!" "Do good to those who persecute you!" We know through our experience of every day how difficult this is and how we avoid even listening to such words. In order to accept this obligation and say to oneself, "I will do it," one must be a person of hope.

Hope is not a human virtue; it is not a virtue to the measure of man: it is a divine virtue. It presupposes in man the measure of God. And it has had this characteristic in us right from the beginning. We have been created to the image of God and this presupposes in us the power of God. And even this is in us. Indeed, John the Evangelist has written: "He gave them the power to become children of God." Hope presupposes in us this divine power, thanks to which we can expect what God himself has promised us through the merits of Christ. We can also aspire with certainty to what is difficult.

The Christian as a man of hope is one who aspires to what is beyond him. And he aspires to it with the certainty that it is not he who does this, but God. The one who has hope always touches with his hand the gift of God in himself or in others or in the community, in individual life or in the collective one. And more often than not, it comes about that God, after the total undoing of man, does what man aspired to but had humanly not succeeded in achieving.

To be able truly to commit our time and capacities to the salvation and sanctification of souls, the Church's first and foremost mission, we must first of all possess certainty and clarity concerning the truths which must be believed and practiced. If we are insecure, uncertain, confused, and contradictory, we cannot build. Especially today it is necessary to possess an enlightened and convinced faith, in order to be able to be enlightening and convincing. The phenomenon of mass "culturalization" requires a profound, clear, and secure faith.

It is necessary that our faith be complete, that it not diminish in us, that it not give in to conformism, to conjectures; that it not become an overly private affair; that it not become separated from what pertains to the very substance of faith, that is, from its confession before all people.

There will be no faith if our heart does not house a question whose answer God alone possesses, or, to put it better, whose answer is God alone.

In order for man to be able to believe in himself, he must believe in God, since man is created in the image and likeness of God. When God is taken away from man, one does not replace him with one's own self but rather one takes away one's own self.

The confession of God is the basis of our human freedom.

Freedom

The Condition of Love

IN our day there is frequent recourse to the principle of religious freedom, and rightly so. This is one of the most basic rights of man . . . But much still remains to be done for the correct functioning of this principle in social, public, national, and international life. And here there is no other road; only this remains: we must free the believing individual from the accusation of alienation. Precisely this accusation is the cause of the great harm done to people in the name of the "progress" of man.

Human dignity can be salvaged only on condition of a just and responsible use of human freedom.

Freedom is the constitutive element of the dignity of the person, uninterruptedly proclaimed and defended by Christian thought. However, we must realize that

Christian freedom is never an end in itself, even though it is inevitably endowed with a finality; it is the means to the true good.

The person is a free being, but his freedom does not signify independence from society.

The person is a free being in the ambit of social life. He makes good use of his freedom when, on the natural base of his inclination to social life, he develops real social values.

Such virtues determine the realization of the common good. The human person cannot develop himself and perfect himself apart from that good.

Freedom is made for love. If it is not used, if it does not profit from love, it becomes precisely something negative and gives us a sense of emptiness. Love binds freedom and saturates it with what by nature attracts the will: the good. Freedom tends toward the good and freedom is a property of the will; that is the reason why we say that freedom is made for love. Above all, thanks to freedom, we in fact participate in the good.

Freedom is offered to us and is conferred on us like a mission. Not only must we possess it, but we must also know how to acquire it. We must construct our own existence by directing it toward the good in an increasing right use of our freedom. This is the real essence, the fundamental task on which depend both the meaning and the value of our whole life.

The thirst for freedom penetrates the heart of every person, and the richer is that heart, the greater is the thirst.

The thirst for freedom permeates the entire history of the human race, the history of peoples and nations, revealing their spiritual maturity and at the same time putting them to the test.

Man has not only the right to work but also the right to a wage. But this is not enough for man. There are more profound rights of the human spirit, freedom of conscience, freedom of opinion, and freedom of religion, which cannot be violated or limited.

True freedom is obtained in proportion to one's conversion to the living and true God; by maturing in charity, one not only frees himself from sin but also discovers and strengthens at the same time the true meaning of his freedom.

The cause of man's spiritual freedom, of his freedom of conscience, of his religious freedom, is a grand human cause—for man in the past and for man today!

Even at the root of obedience and disobedience there is ever the will, that is, freedom: will and freedom in the encounters with the Will.

Love consists in the pledge of one's freedom; it is a gift of self, and "to give oneself" signifies precisely "to limit one's freedom for the advantage of others."

Justice

There Can Be No Love Without Justice

WE know that the values which give us more from the objective viewpoint must also cost us much more subjectively.

Everyone lives and dies with a certain sensation of insatiability for justice, because the earth is not in a position to satisfy completely a being created in the image of God, either in the depths of his person or in the various aspects of his human life.

There can be no love without justice. Love "surpasses" justice, but at the same time it finds its verification in justice. Even the father and mother, loving the child though they do, must be just with him. If justice wavers, love is also endangered.

Justice is a task to be realized which presents itself as ever new to the eyes of every individual and every age.

Human morality cannot be based uniquely on utility; it must tend towards justice, which entails the recognition of the supra-utilitarian value of the person. And in this sense "justice" is clearly contrasted with "utility." Above all, in the sexual sphere it is not enough to ascertain that a certain behaviour is useful; we must be able to say that it is just.

An unjust application of the system of justice on the part of human beings clamors more loudly for final justice, the justice of God himself.

Justice is, according to universal opinion, a cardinal and fundamental virtue because it is indispensable to the order of the coexistence of persons and to their life in common. Speaking of justice toward the creator, we attribute to God the nature of person and recognize the possibility of interpersonal relations between man and God.

It is evident that this opinion presupposes the knowledge and understanding on the one hand of the rights of God and on the other of the duties of man! Both the former and the latter stem above all from the fact that God is the creator of man.

On the day of his death Jesus achieved the most complete communion and solidarity with the whole human family and especially with all those who in the sweep of history have been subjected to injustice, cruelty, and vituperation.

We must strive with all the means at our disposal to achieve this goal: that all forms of injustice which manifest themselves in our day may be subjected to common consideration and really be remedied; and that all people may lead a life worthy of a human being.

Above everything, love must be our guide . . . Love gives strength to justice!

Man began to be unjust in his initial disobedience to his creator. Hence, Jesus became obedient unto death, leaving man his justice like an inexhaustible font for justification before God.

Today the world is pierced by a desperate call for social justice, for justice toward every single person. How many injustices exist today, even in the name of a supposed "justice!"

The human person must be respected! This is the fundamental principle of the exercise of power!

It is the task of the Church to struggle for man, often against man himself! This is how Christ struggled and continues to struggle throughout the ages in the depths of human hearts and human consciences. This is the reason why "the mystery" of every man lies within him. He is man's most profound, ultimate, and even most simple measure.

The desire for happiness is not something superficial, extrinsic, external to our actions. Yet it is not difficult to discover it in these actions and to objectify it: no one can deny that it is forever beating in the depths of the will.

Happiness constitutes the goal of nature.

Happiness, so frequently mentioned by the Gospel, is attained by the medium of perfection. But it cannot be bought "at the price" of perfection.

It is necessary to mature by perfecting ourselves, becoming even better people.

Happiness is already present in this becoming better.

Happiness is not a way.
It is the goal of every way of humanity.

Only with the Gospel of Jesus Christ are we in a position really to free humanity from all slavery and to give ourselves the most profound happiness. Indeed, the Gospel places at the center love rather than hate, equality of all rather than oppression on the part of some, dialogue in peace rather than division in struggles, the human person rather than an abstract ideology, and the promotion of life in all its manifestations rather than its mortification.

Four

The Certainty of the Pastor:
Reflections as Pope

I too will not grow weary of repeating,
As my duty of evangelizing the whole of
    mankind obliges me to do:
"Do not be afraid. Open wide the doors
    for Christ.
To his saving power open the
    boundaries of states,
Economic and political systems,
The vast fields of culture, civilization
    and development."

*Homily of Pope John Paul II
On the Inauguration
of his Pontificate
October 22, 1978*

Discipleship

Being a Christian Today

FOLLOW Christ! You who are single or who are preparing for marriage —Follow Christ! You who are young or old—Follow Christ! You who are sick or aging, who are suffering or in pain. You who feel the need for healing, the need for love, the need for a friend—Follow Christ!

Homily at Boston Common,
Massachusetts

Christians will want to be in the vanguard in favoring ways of life that decisively break with a frenzy of consumerism, exhausting and joyless.

Homily at Yankee Stadium,
New York

Christ came to bring joy; joy to children, joy to parents, joy to families and to friends, joy to workers and to scholars, joy to the sick and to the elderly, joy to all humanity. In a true sense, joy is the keynote of the Christian message and the recurring motif of the Gospels.

Talk in Harlem,
New York City

In a way for us, who know Jesus Christ, human and Christian values are but two aspects of the same reality; the reality of man, redeemed by Christ and called to the fullness of eternal life.

Homily in Logan Circle,
Philadelphia

Man cannot be fully understood without Christ. Or rather, man is incapable of understanding himself fully without Christ. He cannot understand who he is, nor what his true dignity is, nor what his vocation is, nor what his final end is. He cannot understand any of this without Christ.

Homily in Victory Square, Warsaw, Poland

Keep Jesus Christ in your hearts, and you will recognize his face in every human being.

Prayer Service at Shea Stadium New York

You must be strong, dear brothers and sisters. You must be strong with the strength that comes from faith. You must be strong with the strength of faith. You must be faithful. Today more than in any other age you need this strength. You must be strong with the strength of hope, hope that brings the perfect joy of life and does not allow us to grieve the Holy Spirit.

Homily in Cracow, Poland

From this faith in Christ, from the bosom of the church, we are able to serve men and women, our peoples, and to penetrate their culture with the Gospel, to transform hearts, and to make systems and structures more human.

Address to the Latin American Bishops, Puebla, Mexico

Once the Word of God is faithfully proclaimed to the community and is accepted, it brings forth fruits of justice and holiness of life in abundance.

Address to the Bishops of the United States, Chicago

Conversion by its very nature is the condition for that union with God which reaches its greatest expression in the Eucharist. Our union with Christ in the Eucharist presupposes, in turn, that our hearts are set on conversion, that they are pure.

Address to the Bishops of the United States, Chicago

Man lives at the same time both in the world of material values and in that of spiritual values. For the individual living and hoping man, his needs, freedoms and relationships with others never concern one sphere of values alone, but belong to both.

Address to the United Nations, New York

Sometimes, lay men and women do not seem to appreciate to the full the dignity and the vocation that are theirs as lay people. No, there is no such thing as an "ordinary layman," for all of you have been called to conversion through the death and resurrection of Jesus Christ.

Homily in County Limerick, Ireland

The pope expects from you a coherence between your own lives and the life of the church. This coherence implies an awareness of your identity as Catholics, it means giving public witness to it.

*Homily at the Cathedral
in Mexico City*

The church today needs laymen who will give witness to their faith and share her mission in the world, being the ferment of faith, justice and human dignity, in order to build a more human and fraternal world from which we can look up to God.

*Homily at the Cathedral
in Mexico City*

Aware of her great dignity and her magnificent vocation in Christ, the church wishes to go to meet man. The church wishes to respond to the eternal yet ever topical queries of human hearts and human history. For that reason she carried out during the council a work of deeper knowledge of herself, her nature, her mission, her tasks.

Address to parish representatives, Czestochowa, Poland

We must be faithful to the church born once and for all from the plan of God; at the cross, the empty tomb and at Pentecost, which is born not of the people or from reason, but from God. She is born today to build among all men a people willing to grow in faith, hope and fraternal love.

Homily at the Cathedral in Mexico City

The church wishes to place herself at the service of unity among people; she desires to place herself at the service of reconciliation between nations. This belongs to her saving mission. Let us continually open our thoughts and hearts to the peace of which the Lord Jesus so often spoke to the apostles, both before his passion and after his resurrection: "I leave you peace, my peace I give you". (John 14:27).

Homily to Pilgrims of
Silesia, Jasna Gora, Poland

The Christian Family

"I propose to you the option of love"

IT has been said, in a beautiful and profound way, that our God in his innermost mystery is not a Solitary being, but a family, because he hears within himself fatherhood, sonship and the essence of the family, which is love. This love in the Holy Family is the Holy Spirit. The subject of the family is not therefore, foreign to the subject of the Holy Spirit.

Homily at
Puebla, Mexico

Nothing can take the place of the heart of a mother always present and always waiting in the home.

Homily to Polish Miners,
Jasna Gora, Poland

The future of humanity depends in great part on parents and on the family life that they build in their homes. The family is the true measure of the greatness of a nation, just as the dignity of man is the true measure of civilization.

Homily in County Limerick. Ireland

To maintain a joyful family requires much from both parents and the children. Each member of the family has to become, in a special way, the servant of the others and share their burdens (cf. Galatians 6:2, Philippians 2:2). Each one must show concern, not only for his or her own life, but also for the lives of the other members of the family —their needs, their hopes, their ideals.

Homily at the Mall, Washington, DC

Married people must believe in the power of the sacrament to make them holy. They must believe in their vocation to witness through their marriage to the power of Christ's love.

Homily in County Limerick, Ireland

True love and the grace of God can never let marriage become a self-centred relationship of two individuals, living side by side for their own interests.

Homily in County Limerick, Ireland

Follow Christ! You who are married. Share your love and your burdens with each other, respect the human dignity of your spouse, accept joyfully the life that God gives through you; make your marriage stable and secure for your children's sake.

Homily at Boston Common, Massachusetts

Every child is a unique and unrepeatable gift of God, with the right to a loving and united family.

Homily at the Mall, Washington, DC

I wish to express the joy that we all find in children, the springtime of life, the anticipation of the future history of each of our present earthly homelands.

Address to the United Nations, New York

Concern for the child, even before birth, from the first moment of conception and then throughout the years of infancy and youth, is the primary and fundamental test of the relationship of one human being to another.

Address to the United Nations, New York

Dear young people. Do not be afraid of honest effort and honest work; do not be afraid of the truth. With Christ's help, and through prayer, you can answer His call, resisting temptations and fads, and every form of mass manipulation. Open your hearts to the Christ of the Gospels—to his love and his truth and his joy.

Homily at Boston Common, Massachusetts

When you wonder about the mystery of yourself, look to Christ who gives you the meaning of life.

When you wonder what it means to be a mature person, look to Christ who is the fullness of humanity.

And when you wonder about your role in the future of the world and of the United States, look to Christ. Only in Christ will you fulfill your potential as an American citizen and as a citizen of the world community.

Talk to youth in Madison Square Garden, New York

Again and again I find in young people the joy and enthusiasm of life, a searching for truth and for the deeper meaning of the existence that unfolds before them in all its attraction and potential.

Homily at Boston Common, Massachusetts

Dear young people. You and I and all of us together make up the church, and we are convinced that only in Christ do we find real love, and the fullness of life. And so I invite you today to look to Christ.

Talk to youth in Madison Square Garden, New York

Faced with problems and disappointments, many people will try to escape from their responsibility, escape in selfishness, escape in sexual pleasure, escape in drugs, escape in violence, escape in indifference and cynical attitudes. But today, I propose to you the option of love, which is the opposite of escape. If you really accept that love from Christ, it will lead you to God.

Homily at Boston Common, Massachusetts

Human Justice

A World of Peace and Freedom

THE pope wants to be your voice, the voice of those who cannot speak or who are silenced, to be the conscience of the consciences, the invitation to action, in order to make up for lost time, a time that is frequently one of prolonged suffering and of unfulfilled hopes.

Talk to peasants,
Cuilapan, Mexico

And so, what better wish can I express for every nation and the whole of mankind, and for all the children of the world than a better future in which respect for human rights will become a complete reality throughout the third millennium, which is drawing near.

Speech at the United Nations,
New York

This voice of the church, echoing the voice of human conscience, and which did not cease to make itself heard down through the centuries in the midst of the most varied social and cultural systems and conditions, deserves and needs to be heard in our time also, when the growing wealth of a few runs parallel to the growing poverty of the masses.

Address to the Latin American Bishops, Puebla, Mexico

Is it enough to put man in a different uniform, arm him with the apparatus of violence? Is it enough to impose on him an ideology in which human rights are subjected to the demands of the system, completely subjected to them, so as in practice not to exist at all?

Address at Auschwitz in Poland

A human person is a free and responsible being. He or she is a knowing and responsible subject. He or she can and must, with the power of personal thought, come to know the truth. He or she can and must choose and decide.

Homily in
Cracow, Poland

Freedom thus acquires a deeper meaning when it is referred to the human person. It concerns in the first place the relation of man to himself. Every human person, endowed with reason, is free when he is the master of his own actions, when he is capable of choosing that goal which is in conformity with reason, and therefore with his own human dignity.

Homily in Logan Circle,
Philadelphia

When freedom is used to dominate the weak, to squander natural resources and energy, and to deny basic necessities to people, we will stand up and reaffirm the demands of justice and social love.

*Homily at the Mall,
Washington, DC*

When the sick, the aged or the dying are abandoned in loneliness, we will stand up and proclaim that they are worthy of love, care and respect.

*Homily at the Mall,
Washington, DC*

Freedom in justice will bring a new dawn of hope for the present generation as it has done before; for the homeless, for the unemployed, for the aging, for the sick and the handicapped, for the migrants and the undocumented workers, for all who hunger for human dignity in this land and in the world.

*Talk at Battery Park,
New York*

How serious is any threat to human rights? Any violation of them, even in a "peace situation," is a form of warfare against humanity.

Speech at the United Nations, New York

In the final analysis the moral order is built up by means of human beings. This order consists of a large number of tests, each one a test of faith and of character. From every victorious test the moral order is built up. From every failed test moral disorder grows.

Homily at Cracow, Poland

God's justice and peace cry out to bear fruit in human works of justice and peace, in all the spheres of actual life. When we Christians make Jesus Christ the center of our feelings and thoughts we do not turn away from people and their needs. On the contrary, we are caught up in the movement of the Son, who came among us, who became one of us; we are caught in the movement of the Holy Spirit, who visits the poor, calms fevered hearts, binds up wounded hearts, warms cold hearts and gives us the fullness of his gifts.

Homily at Yankee Stadium,
New York

The reason I have called attention to the dimension constituted by spiritual realities is my concern for the cause of peace, peace which is built up by men and women uniting around what is most fully and profoundly human, around what raises them above the world about them and determines their undestructible grandeur—indestructible in spite of the death to which everyone on earth is subject.

Speech at the United Nations,
New York

Jesus does not merely give us peace. He gives us his peace accompanied by his justice. He *is* peace and justice. He becomes our peace and our justice.

Homily at Yankee Stadium, New York

Jesus came and began to share our human condition, its sufferings and difficulties, even death, before transforming the daily life of the people. He talked to the masses of the poor, to liberate them from sin, to open their eyes to a horizon of enlightenment and fill them with joy and hope. He does the same today. Christ is present in your church, in your homes, in your hearts, in your life. Open the doors to him.

Address to Migrant Workers, Monterrey, Mexico

The parable of the rich man and Lazarus must always be present in our memory; it must form our conscience. Christ demands openness to our brothers and sisters in need—openness from the rich, the affluent, the economically advanced; openness to the poor, the underdeveloped and the disadvantaged. Christ demands an openness that is more than benign attention, more than token actions or half-hearted efforts that leave the poor as destitute as before or even more so.

Homily at Yankee Stadium, New York

In the name of the solidarity that binds us all together in a common humanity, I again proclaim the dignity of every human person; the rich man and Lazarus are both human beings. (applause) both of them equally created in the image and likeness of God, both of them equally redeemed by Christ, at a great price, the price of "the precious Blood of Christ (1 Pt 1:19)."

Homily at Yankee Stadium, New York

The poor of the United States and of the world are your brothers and sisters in Christ. You must never be content to leave them just the crumbs from the feast. You must take of your substance, and not just of your abundance, in order to help them. And you must treat them like guests at your family table.

Homily at Yankee Stadium, New York

Human Dignity

The Love of Life

I DO not hesitate to proclaim before you and before the world that all human life—from the moment of conception and through all subsequent stages—is sacred, because human life is created in the image and likeness of God. Nothing surpasses the greatness of dignity of a human person.

Homily at the Mall, Washington, DC

All human beings ought to value every person for his or her uniqueness as a creature of God, called to be a brother or sister of Christ by reason of the incarnation and the universal Redemption. For us, the sacredness of human life is based on these premises. And it is on these same premises

125

that there is based our celebration of life
—all human life.

Homily at the Mall,
Washington, DC

Human life is precious because it is the gift
of a God whose love is infinite; and when
God gives life, it is forever. Life is also
precious because it is the expression and the
fruit of love. This is why life should spring
up within the setting of marriage, and why
marriage and the partners' love for one
another should be marked by generosity in
self-giving.

Homily at the Mall,
Washington, DC

Work to improve your human life. But
don't stop there. Make yourselves ever
more worthy morally and religiously. Do
not harbor feelings of hate or of violence,
but rather gaze toward the Lord of all, who
to each one gives the reward which his acts
deserve. The church is with you and en-

courages you to live as sons of God, united to Christ, under the gaze of our Blessed Mother.

Talk to peasants,
Cuilapan, Mexico

Human-Christian values triumph by subjecting political and economic considerations to human dignity, by making them serve the cause of man—every person created by God, every brother and sister redeemed by Christ.

Homily at Logan Circle,
Philadelphia

In the Gospel Jesus Christ tells us, "You shall love your neighbor as yourself" (Mt 22:39). This commandment of the Lord must be your inspiration in forming true human relationships among yourselves, so that nobody will ever feel alone or unwanted, or much less, rejected, despised or hated. Jesus himself will give you the power of fraternal love. And every neighborhood, every block, every street will become a true community because you will want it so, and Jesus will help you to bring it about.

Prayer Service at
Shea Stadium in New York

To each one of you I say therefore, heed the call of Christ when you hear him saying to you, "Follow me, walk in my path, stand by my side, remain in my love." There is a choice to be made, a choice for Christ and his way of life and his commandment of love.

Homily at Boston Common,
Massachusetts

The message of love that Christ brought is always important, always relevant. It is not difficult to see how today's world despite its beauty and grandeur, despite the conquests of science and technology, despite the refined and abundant material goods that it offers is yearning for more truth, for more love, for more joy. And all of this is found in Christ and in his way of life.

Homily at Boston Common, Massachusetts

Above all, a city needs a soul if it is to become a true home for human beings. You, the people, must give it this soul. And how do you do this? By loving each other. Love for each other must be the hallmark of your lives.

Prayer Service at Shea Stadium in New York

I want to meet you and tell you all—men and women of all creeds and ethnic origins, children and youth, fathers and mothers, the sick and the elderly—that God loves you, that he has given you a dignity as human beings that is beyond compare. I want to tell everyone that the pope is your friend and a servant of your humanity.

Homily at Boston Common, Massachusetts

Real love is demanding. I would fail in my mission if I did not clearly tell you so.

Homily at Boston Common, Massachusetts

Our celebration of life forms part of the celebration of the Eucharist. Our Lord and Savior, through his death and resurrection, has become for us "the bread of life" and the pledge of eternal life. In him we find the courage, perseverance and inventiveness which we need to promote and defend life within our families and throughout the world.

Homily at the Mall, Washington, DC

Brothers and sisters and friends, do not give in to despair, but work together, take the steps possible for you in the task of increasing your dignity, unite your efforts towards the goals of human and moral advancement. And do not forget that God has your lives in his care, goes with you, calls you to better things, calls you to overcome.

Talk in the South Bronx
New York

Christ Our Bread

Work and the Gift of the Earth

CHRISTIANITY and the church have no fear of the world of work. They have no fear of the system based on work. The Pope has no fear of men at work. They have always been particularly close to him. He has come from their midst. He has come from the quarries of Yakrzowck, from the Solvay furnaces in Borck Falecki, and then from Nowa Huta. Through all these surroundings, through his own experience of work, I make bold to say that the pope learned the Gospel anew.

Homily at the Shrine of the Cross, Mogila, Poland

Work is not a burden, it is a blessing of God, which calls man to subdue the earth and transform it so that with human intelligence and effort, He will continue his creative and divine work. I want to tell you with all my soul and strength that I am hurt by unemployment; I am deeply hurt by injustice; I am hurt by conflicts; I am hurt by ideologies of hate and violence that are not evangelical and cause so many wounds to contemporary humanity.

Address to workers,
Guadalajara, Mexico

Work is also the fundamental dimension of man's life on earth. Work has for man a significance that is not merely technical but ethical. It can be said that man "subdues" the earth when by his behavior he becomes its master, not its slave, and also the master and not the slave of work.

Homily to Polish Miners,
Jasna Gora, Poland

In every human work prayer sets up a reference to God the creator and redeemer and it also contributes to complete "humanization" of work.

*Homily to Polish Miners,
Jasna Gora, Poland*

Do not let yourselves be seduced by the temptation to think that man can fully find himself by denying God, erasing prayer from his life and remaining only a worker, deluding himself that what he produces can on its own fill the needs of the human heart. "Man shall not live by bread alone" (Mt 4:4).

*Homily to Polish Miners,
Jasna Gora, Poland*

Farmers everywhere provide bread for all humanity, but it is Christ alone who is the bread of life. He alone satisfies the deepest hunger of humanity.

*Homily at Living History Farms,
Des Moines, Iowa*

The land is God's gift entrusted to people from the very beginning. It is God's gift, given by a loving creator as a means of sustaining the life which he had created. But the land is not only God's gift; it is also man's responsibility.

Homily at Living History Farms,
Des Moines, Iowa

Man, himself created from the dust of the earth (cf Gen. 3:7), was made its master (cf Gen. 1:26). In order to bring forth fruit, the land would depend upon the genius and skillfulness, the sweat and the toil of the people to whom God would entrust it.

Homily at Living History Farms,
Des Moines, Iowa

The rural world possesses enviable human and religious richness; a deep love of family, a sense of friendship, help to the needy, deep humanism, love of peace and community, religious awareness, confidence and openness with God, cultivation of the love of the Virgin Mary and many other virtues.

*Talk to Peasants,
Cuilapan, Mexico*

We shall create a world that is almost un-inhabitable if we look only to *further gain* and do not think primarily of the person of the worker as a human being and a child of God who is called to an eternal destiny; if we do not think of helping him to a *fuller existence*.

*Address to Migrant Workers,
Monterrey, Mexico*

This is the great and fundamental right of man; the right to work and the right to land. Although the development of the economy may take us in another direction, although progress may be evaluated on the basis of industrialization, although today's genera-tion may leave en masse the countryside and the work of the fields, nevertheless the right to land does not cease to constitute the basis of a sound economy and sociology.

Homily at Nowy Targ, Poland

Only Christ can create one anew, and this new creation finds its beginning only in his cross and resurrection. In Christ alone all creation is restored to its proper order. Therefore, I say: "Come all of you to Christ. He is the bread of life. Come to Christ and you will never be hungry again."

Homily at Living History Farms, Des Moines, Iowa

Large Print Inspirational Books from Walker

Would you like to be on our Large Print mailing list? Please send your name and address to:

B. Walker
Walker and Company
720 Fifth Avenue
New York, NY 10019

A Book of Hours

Elizabeth Yates

The Alphabet of Grace

Frederick Buechner

The Adventure of Spiritual Healing

Michael Drury

A Certain Life: Contemporary Meditations on the Way of Christ

Herbert O'Driscoll

A Gathering of Hope

Helen Hayes

Getting Through the Night: Finding Your Way After the Loss of a Loved One

Eugenia Price

Inner Healing: God's Great Assurance

Theodore Dobson

Instrument of Thy Peace

Alan Paton

The Irrational Season

Madeleine L'Engle

Jonathan Livingston Seagull

Richard Bach

Living Simply Through the Day

Tilden Edwards

The Power of Positive Thinking

Norman Vincent Peale

The Touch of the Earth

Jean Hersey

Gift From the Sea

Anne Morrow Lindbergh

A Grief Observed

C.S. Lewis

A Guide to Christian Meditation

Marilyn Morgan Helleberg

Up From Grief

Bernardine Kreis and Alice Pattie

Walking With Loneliness

Paula Ripple

The Way of the Wolf

Martin Bell

Who Will Deliver Us?

Paul Zahl

With Open Hands

Henri Nouwen

Words of Certitude

Pope John Paul II

Words to Love By

Mother Teresa

The Sacred Journey

Frederick Buechner

Something Beautiful for God

Malcolm Muggeridge

Strength to Love

Martin Luther King, Jr.

To God Be the Glory

Billy Graham and
Corrie Ten Boom